I'm not
that
kind of
girl

300

Dedicated to
my father

Other books by

Susan Polis Schutz

Come Into the Mountains, Dear Friend
I Want to Laugh, I Want to Cry
Peace Flows from the Sky
Someone Else to Love

I'm not that kind of girl

a collection of poetry by
Susan Polis Schutz
designed and illustrated by
Stephen Schutz

Blue Mountain Arts T.M.
Boulder, Colorado

The following works have been published for the first
time in this book: "I know that we are separated,"
"Sitting around," "Many relationships," "The
darkness hides," "We walked along the sand,"
"Thunder, Lightning," "Little one year old son,"
"My Little Son," "An Education" and "Painting the
Truths."

In addition, selections have been made from poems
which have previously appeared on notecards,
scrolls and books by Susan Polis Schutz: "Man is
forced to," Copyright © Continental Publications,
1971. "Music touches feelings," Copyright ©
Continental Publications, 1973. "Walking down a
crowded street," Copyright © Continental
Publications, 1974.
"Because our relationship,"
"What is love?"
"Some people are always alone,"
"Sometimes you do not,"
"You are a free person," Copyright © Continental
Publications, 1975.

Library of Congress Number: 76-024989
ISBN: 0-88396-017-6

First Printing: September, 1976
Second Printing: July, 1977
Third Printing: February, 1978
Printed in the United States of America.

 **Blue Mountain Arts** inc.
P.O. Box 4549   Boulder, Colorado 80306

CONTENTS

CHILDREN OF NATURE

I'M NOT THAT KIND OF GIRL

INTRODUCTION

I write to express my feelings. Many of you
have written to me about how you
identify with my feelings, and thanking me for
writing my poems. I would like to
thank all of you. It is always nice to discover
that, indeed, you are not alone. There
are people who understand.

I'm Not That Kind of Girl is a collection of
my poems taken from my first three books,
*Come Into the Mountains, Dear Friend; Peace
Flows from the Sky;* and *I Want to Laugh,
I Want to Cry,* as well as sixteen new poems.
Each of the six chapters is about different
feelings I have had on specific subjects such
as love, friendship, society, nature,
creativity and women.

The sensitive airbrush and pen and ink
drawings are created by Stephen Schutz.
Stephen reads my poem, and thinks about it for
several days. Then he creates the mood
of my poem with his illustration. I am proud to
have Stephen add such a beautiful dimension
to my poems. I am also proud to love him.

And I am proud to share my thoughts
with you. Thank you for listening.

Susan Polis Schutz
June 24, 1976

We share
rather
than control
each other's lives

Because our relationship
is based on
honesty and
fairness
there is no
need to test
each other.
It is so
wonderful
to find someone
whom I
don't need
to play games
with
and who lives
up to everything that
I consider
important, right and
beautiful.

I know that
we are separated
by many
days walking
but distance
can never
weaken our
relationship
for what
is in our
minds and hearts
is stronger
than any
outside force
and when we are
together again
our relationship
will be
that much more
intense and beautiful

What is love?
I only know that
I feel warmth
and happiness
when I am near you.
I feel a complete truthfulness
and understanding
when I talk to you.
I feel a deep involvement
and interest
when I listen to you.
I feel as though I am
the sun, the moon, the trees
when we are together.
Is this love?
And isn't this
better than love?

Sitting around
reading pensively
quietly discussing
our thoughts
gazing into the sun
thinking

the waves slap
loudly against
the sand
people all around
drinking martinis
surfing, playing and
laughing
people happy
to be with happy people

but I like to always be
by myself, always
with
you

Many relationships
are fine
but I'm tired of
trying to explain
myself

I like
saying what I mean
and acting the way I feel
I like the truth

What excites
me in our relationship is that
I am able to be
my real self, truthfully
to your real self

The darkness hides
the mountains in silhouettes
we are together
peacefully
we have nothing
to hide from each other
under the night moon

The sun breaks over
the snow-capped mountain ranges
we look at each other
honestly
we are able to expose our
whole selves to each other
in the light of the day
every day
every night

Some people are always alone
I was, until I met you
Some people can not trust others
I could not, until I met you
Some people are not able to appreciate
the flowers and trees
I could not, until I met you
Some people are always dissatisfied
I was, until I met you
Some people can not find peace
I could not, until I met you
Some people are never able to
experience a sincere love
I could not,
until I met
you

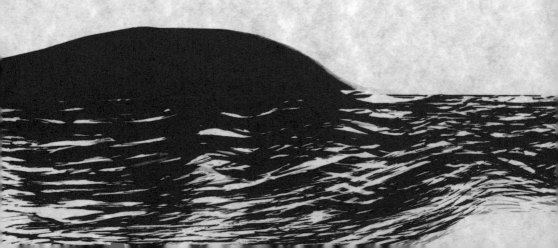

We walked along the sand
wondering why our relationship
is so successful in a time
when most are not
we thought about
how we respect each other
how we give each other freedom
and how we have fun together

We stopped to rest on a huge moss rock
and continued to think
how honest we are with each other
how we tell each other every feeling
we have, whether good or bad
how we never have to pretend
to each other

We ran back to the shore, holding hands
still not knowing why our
relationship is so beautiful
but very thankful that it is

Sometimes you do not
say anything
and I know exactly
what you are thinking
    Sometimes you
    see something beautiful
    and it is as though I
    see it too
Sometimes you
touch something
and by holding your hand
I feel like I
touch it also
    Sometimes you
    learn something interesting
    and by listening to you
    I learn it also
Always when you are
happy, I am happy
because you
are a part of me
and my life is
intermingled with your
life

I sit
in this chair
in my house
in this city
far away
from you.
I vividly
picture you
sitting
in that chair
in your house
in your city.
And though
I miss you
desperately
we are
together
in my thoughts.

When lying beside you
it is strange and away from reality.
I am surrounded by flowers, and you
are all that nature is.

With you there
and me here
I have had no one
to discuss little things with
like how the dew feels on the grass
or big things like
what's going on in the world

I have been lonely
talking and thinking to myself
I now realize how essential it is
to have someone
to share oneself with

Sometimes
when I am
sitting alone
I think of you
Sometimes
when I am
out with a lot
of people
I think of you
Always when I
want to talk to
someone
I think of you

Our relationship
is so strong
because we
treat each other
as equals in
every aspect of
life
and because
we are completely
truthful with
each other
in every word and
thought

Everywhere rose mountains of sand
making us very tiny
The night wind drew us together
and the crackling fire warmed our feet
We were in the sky
or we were on a desert in the biblical days
and you were Moses climbing the mountain
surrounded by peaceful barrenness and love

How beautiful it is
when acting and being are one
No crying when laughing
No sadness when happiness

My emotions have been softened
My body possessed
I am independent
but captured

You are mine
and I am yours
in love

I am I
and you are you
in thought

Independently
we share our lives
together

I am so happy with you
I can discuss all my thoughts, or
I don't have to say anything
You always understand.

I am so relaxed with you
I don't need to pretend
I don't need to look good
You accept me for what I am.

I am so strong with you
I depend on you for love
but I live my own life
You give me extra confidence to succeed.

Thunder, lightning
sun is gone; clouds are red
ground is fed

Clouds disappear
land is dry
rainbowed sky

Today we celebrated
the birthday of our love.
We rode our motorcycle
down an old dirt road
on the side of a still pure lake.
The clouds touched our heads
on the long bumpy cliff.
Twenty miles away from life
we stopped.

Seven years ago we met.
Six years ago we loved.
And now, still, we love more.
Our bodies met
outside in the sand.
The air sent a chill
to wake us
from our fantasy.
Us
the sun
the lake
the sand
forever.

I sit here
bored
I don't feel like talking
to the people here
I don't feel like looking
at this place anymore

I sit here
lonely
realizing that it's not
people or places that
make me happy
It's you

It's nighttime
I see your face
in the stars
I feel your gentleness
with the swaying of the leaves

It's nighttime
cold and dark
but the moon
warms my heart
with the thought
that we will
be together again soon

A house
is a place where one lives
as is a
basement.
But this house
is special.
High in the sky
our house sits
on a large mountain
looking out on the
whole city.
Lights blink below
like a year round Christmas
From the deck
we inhale
the pine tree air
while watching
the twinkling magic.
Our neighbors,
the deer, cactus and birds
create a very
peaceful family.
Sitting in our windowy
living room
we are on
top of the world
and so far away
from things.
A house
is a place
where one lives.
But our house
is a place where one loves.

Alone
we are
two separate
individuals
trying to survive
Together
we are
strength
and
truth
and
nature
in a world
of love

I am so proud
as you walk so straight down the road
stopping to pat little children's heads

I am so proud
when you hike in the woods
and feed stray animals

I am so proud
when you look at me so softly
and the whole world can
see your feelings

I am so proud
to exchange myself with you
and for us to become one

When you are not with me
my life is so different
I barely function in my daily tasks
and do just what is expected of me
and no more

When you are near me
I am a complete person
involved in all my work
I am a burst of life
looking forward to
each new second

In the morning
when the sun
is just starting to light the day
I am awakened
and my first thoughts are of you

At night
I stare at the dark trees
silhouetted against the quiet stars
I am entranced into a complete peacefulness
and my last thoughts are of you

Little one year old son

Camping in the wilderness
I rocked him in my arms
he blinked, smiled
and fell into a deep sleep
Little one year old son
he stands and smiles
he plays and smiles
he crawls and smiles
he does mischief and smiles
He is a happy baby
whom we so dearly love

Little one year old son
thin blonde hair with one curl on his neck
inquisitive gentle sparkling eyes
red puffy cheeks and tiny straight nose
small pear-shaped lips always ready to kiss
He is a beautiful baby
whom we so dearly love

Little one year old son
so sensitive to love
so knowing of hurt
so aware of all that is beautiful
so excited by life
so able to express how he feels

Little one year old son
he is an angel
whom we so dearly love

My Little Son

My little son
to walk
and play with him
to talk
and listen to him
to understand
and comfort him
to love
and laugh with him
to teach
and learn from him
to watch him grow
and grow
and grow
as I grow and grow
beside him

Air so fresh and clear
The silence echoes the chirping of the crickets
We're holding hands
watching not to step on the ants today

Our hearts are open
because right now, everything appears
        so peaceful
It's a beautiful day
and it has temporarily overwhelmed us

I want to wake him
and say thank you
thank you for
knowing me

I want to wake him
and say thank you
thank you for
understanding me

I want to wake him
and say thank you
thank you for
making me so happy

I want to wake him
and say thank you
thank you for transforming me
into erotic delirium

But there he sleeps
so quiet and peaceful
I'll just kiss him softly
and thank him tomorrow

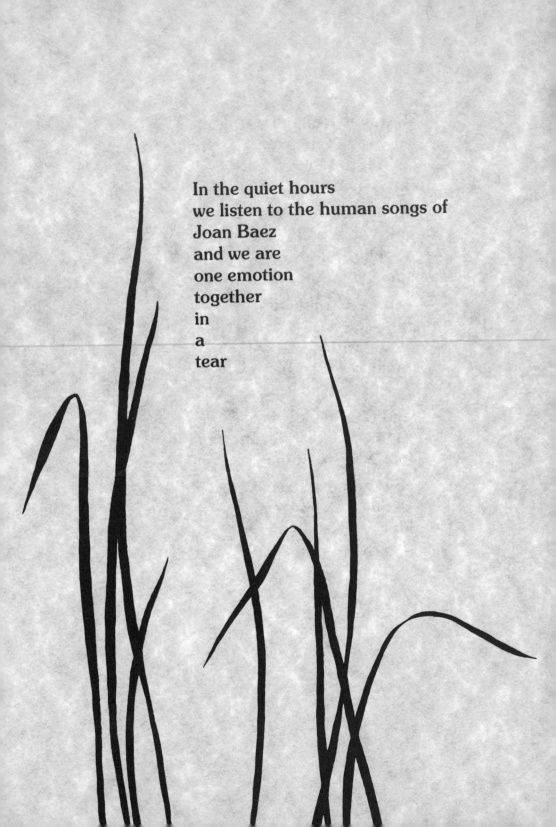

In the quiet hours
we listen to the human songs of
Joan Baez
and we are
one emotion
together
in
a
tear

Our souls touch
Our hearts feel
Our bodies meet
and we are
one
complete
allness

Sometimes I wake up ecstatic
realizing that I am me
different from everyone else
yet the same
I look me
I think me
I feel me
But me alone is not complete
so I have joined you

When I am working
you are with me
When I am playing
you are with me
When I am alone
you are with me

Even though we may be apart
you are always
with me

If you have a goal in life
that takes a lot of energy
that requires a lot of work
that incurs a great deal of interest
and that is a challenge to you

You will always look
forward to waking up
to see what the new day brings

If you have a person in your life
that understands you completely
that shares your ideas
that trusts you
and believes in everything you do

You will always look
forward to the night
because you will never be lonely

Your heart is my heart
   Your truth is my truth
      Your feeling is my feeling

But the real strength of our love
is that we share rather than
control each other's lives

You know how I feel

I haven't seen you in awhile
yet I often imagine
all your expressions

I haven't spoken to you recently
but many times
I hear your thoughts

Good friends must not always
be together
It is the feeling of oneness
when distant
that proves a lasting friendship

I go out
all the time
with so many
people
but when I
need someone
to understand me
it is not these
acquaintances to whom
I turn
It is always
to you,
my true friend

Someone
to talk with
to dance with
to sing with
to eat with
to laugh with
to cry with
to think with
to understand
Someone
to be my friend

Man is forced to
be alone by the very
nature of society. But
if you meet a person
who is not envious,
who loves and believes
in other than himself,
then to this rare person
offer a lifetime
of friendship.

Our friendship has taken on new meaning
In the long time since
        we traded comic books and
            shared the same heroes.

Now we rarely see each other,
but when we do meet,
we sit for hours discussing our lives
and it is as though we never parted.

It is comforting to know
that whatever happens, whether good or bad,
there is a friend who will understand.

You
are
a
free
person.
I am so happy
because in your
freedom, you
chose me to
be your friend.

A man is only complete
when he has a true friend
to understand him,
to share all his
passions and sorrows with,
and to stand by him
throughout his life.

Knowing that you are always here to understand and accept me helps me get along in the confused world. If every person could have someone just like you, the world would become a peaceful garden.

There is no need
for an outpouring of
words to explain oneself
to a friend.
Friends understand each
other's thoughts even before
they are spoken.

When a person has a real friend, he learns not only to appreciate another human being, but he also learns to understand himself better.

When someone cares
it is easier to speak
it is easier to listen
it is easier to play
it is easier to work

When someone cares
it is easier to laugh

Though we
drifted apart in distance
I always
think of you as being right here
Though we have different interests
our experiences are still the same
and though we
have many new friends
it is our old and
continuous friendship
that means the most to me

Many a sun set
since I last saw you—
when we played
in our tree hut
and planned our lives.
You, a teacher-to-be,
Me, a writer-to-be.

Now, fifteen autumns later,
we meet.
You, smelling of lemon cosmetics, dressed
                    in the latest fashion,
Me, with my faded jeans and turtleneck.
You, with three little children that look
                    just like you,
Me, with my three unpublished manuscripts.
You, with your shiny dishwasher and
                    wall to wall carpeting,
Me, with my paper plates. . . .

But you living your life through others
and me living my own life with others.

We parted with tears,
each looking at the other with pity.
Knowing that we had very little left in common,
we both wished that perhaps there was
enough to keep our friendship alive,
even if just to meet each other occasionally
                    to see
how another segment of the world lives.

You know how I feel
You listen to how I think
You understand . . .
You're
my
friend.

We need
to feel more

An Education

Wasted seconds, minutes, hours
    sitting, listening, sighing,
    thumping, pounding, crying,
    tapping, choking, dying.

Empty voices echoing
    so much nothing,
    drilling, shrilling, killing.

My mind is escaping
their detestable faking

    Ahhh . . . to be in my own world
        into which they cannot penetrate.

I stare out my window
and 10,000 windows stare back
families, lovers, roommates in each apartment
involved in their own fictions

Lights blinking — airplanes, bridges, cars
everyone is running
you cannot even see the stars

I wonder who lives in the window
with the flowers
and what are they thinking
as they gaze through their glass

How can I stand out so as
not to be just another
window shadow?

If you want to live in the country
If you want to live in the city
If you want to be a carpenter
If you want to be an artist
Do it!

If you want to tell someone they are right
If you want to tell someone they are wrong
If you want to tell someone you are happy
If you want to tell someone you are sorry
Tell it!

Do you like to dress neat?
Do you like to dress sloppy?
Do you want to have long hair?
Do you want to have short hair?

                              Look it.

Do you want to love men?
Do you want to love women?
Do you want a lot of friends?
Do you want to be alone?

                              Do it.

If you feel like screaming
If you feel like laughing
If you feel like talking
If you feel like being silent

                              Feel it.

Do it.
Tell it.
Look it.
Feel it.
Now.
It's your only chance.
Live the life you dream.
Dream the life you live.

Men are told by society that
they always have to be strong
and put on a tough exterior
to block out all sensitive "unmanly" feelings

It is drilled into men from birth
that they are leaders
that they must achieve
that they must succeed in a career
Men are judged their whole lives
by the power they have
and how much they earn

I would hate to have
such overwhelming pressure
threaten my entire life

I see a little boy being bullied by bigger boys
tears come to my eyes
I see New York City with all its action
and I get so excited that I stammer
I smell rubbing alcohol which reminds me of hospitals
and I cry for all the sick people
I meet people whom I love
and I love them openly
I am so glad that I have learned not to
hide my feelings

Down in the city
the noise of cars rumble
fire engines squeal
people yell

Up here in the mountains
birds sing
dogs bark
deer play
and I sit here peacefully
thinking how insane city life is

New York City is the
most interesting place to live
Millions of people
bumping into you
each with an interesting story to share
A world center for
industry, publishers,
stock market, museums,
concerts, plays, television,
and most
everything else

There is always
something new to discover
or someone new to meet
One's mind is always challenged
New York City is an international city
a world of its own

If you could take the Colorado outdoors
and put it in New York City
then you'd have a perfect city
But since you can't,
New York City remains a place for your mind,
but not for your soul

PAINTING THE TRUTHS—1967

When you enter Kindergarten, you are told that Mommy is going to the store for a while, and that you are to play with the smiling lady standing near the piano.

Advancing through the primary grades, you are taught such important facts as—"George Washington never told a lie; you were born from a stalk; spinach makes you strong and muscular; and that you must be nice around Christmas time so Santa will give you gifts . . . "

The primary grades end, and though you have seen many babies, you never saw a stalk; and you bitterly ate spinach every day, but with daily muscle measurements the bulge did not increase; and you saw three Santa Clauses in one day . . . but you quickly forget these oppositions and move upward on the educational path to junior high school.

Here you learn that there is no Santa, and your baby brother did not come from a stalk, HUMPH! Well, now that you are older, people will tell you the truth — — "Never ever start a sentence with and or but; smoking stunts your growth; the American government is gloriously infallible; and the enemy is the (we shouldn't even say the frightening word) Communists; the number one singing group is brilliant and completely dedicated to the betterment of music (as quoted by your trusted magazine) . . . "

continued

You are now in high school. What a fool you have been! Your teachers' fear of a stunted growth should no longer exist, for what you now smoke makes you very high. You've read books by Pulitzer Prize authors, and their using and or but at the beginnings of sentences did not seem to affect the judges. The number one singing group split up because they could not divide their profits equally. The government's been having troubles, and to top it off, the smiling lady whom you played with in Kindergarten had a nervous breakdown. What's it all about???

You enter college, and for four years you take notes, cram, test, dance, drink, smoke, take notes, cram, test, dance, drink, smoke, eat, sleep, probe, dance, smoke, experiment — passing through all moral, immoral, and finally amoral stages, ranging from a pensive philosopher to a free living neurotic.

As your college career so quickly terminates, you are confronted with more confusing realizations — —

Your President is assassinated. Your strict upbringing is in direct conflict with what's happening. The most crucial social problem which concerned your parents, teenage clubs and magazines is, "Should I kiss him on the first date," when what's happening is that 85% of the female graduating class already are living with their boyfriends. Members of Congress are corrupt, and doctors are getting ten dollars for a three-minute visit where they prescribe aspirins and tetracyclin. Emcees on T.V. are getting rich due to their sardonic "Yahoo" personalities. People swear that they are not prejudiced because "some of their best friends are . . . " We are spending billions of dollars to kill people and to fly us to the moon, but to get enough money to do research on cancer, one must stay awake for 48 hours begging for contributions on a telethon.

You now have a college degree. And for the first time, you really know nothing. An understanding is incomprehensible in a world built on hiding and painting the truths.

Walking down a crowded street
listening to the wandering musician
has a different feeling
than going to a crowded concert hall

The street player
is more earthy
more in touch
with reality
You can identify
with the street player
While the concert player
is untouchable

We need to feel more
to understand others.
We need to love more
to be loved back.
We need to cry more
to cleanse ourselves.
We need to laugh more
to enjoy ourselves.
We need to see more
other than our own little fantasies.
We need to hear more
and listen to the needs of others.
We need to give more
and take less.
We need to share more
and own less.
We need to look more
and realize that we are not so different
                    from one another.
We need to create a world where
all can peacefully live the life they choose.

Music
makes me
love

Everyone wants to know
where poets write.
They picture the poet
sitting in front of a fire
in a rustic log cabin,
or perhaps in front of
a beautiful oak roll-top desk
in a large room with stained glass
windows.

If I told you I write
on the beach
and in the mountains,
you would like me

If I told you I write
under the hair dryer,
in the shower
and in bed
you would dislike me
because I'm destroying
the glamorous myth of poets.

The truth is,
a poet writes
everywhere,
anywhere or
anytime she is inspired.

Music transcends all barriers
among people
Slow soft songs
    eyes are sad and misty
Fast songs
    eyes are sparkling
Old familiar songs
    eyes are dreamy
Witty songs
    eyes are laughing

No matter who we are
or where we come from
when listening to music
we are all one

Please people
listen to him.
He is
making
music.
He is
trying to
entertain you.
He is
showing you
his soul.
Please people
listen to him.

When love is beautiful
the poem about love
should be beautiful
but if it is
there are those people
who call it "light and soppy"

When the sky is clear blue
and the mountain air crisp
the poem about nature
should be beautiful
but if it is
there are those people
who call it "light and soppy"

When the birds sing
and the flowers bloom
the poem about life
should be beautiful
but if it is
there are those people
who call it "light and soppy"

But when
love is unrequited
and suicide contemplated
these same people
call the poem a work of art

Something is very wrong
when people are so
ashamed of beautiful feelings
that they call them "light and soppy"
while being so proud of anguish
that they equate it
with being an intellectual

Something is very sad
about people who feel this way
(or at least say they do)
they will never be
free from themselves
to experience any kind
of beauty in their lives

When you are a struggling
straggling young artist
People love you

When you can not afford breakfast
and live in a dirty basement
People say what a dedicated artist you are

When you spend your time creating
and have no time left for friends
People say that you are a true artist

When you sell your first creation
everyone cheers
When you sell your second creation
everyone is happy

But, as your creations gain recognition
and your name is known
Many of these same people hate you

Fame grows and there is a real
demand for your work
Some people say you are now commercial

And many of the same people say
"an overnight success," "doesn't deserve it,"
"creates for the public,"
"not a true artist at all"

They forget the years of struggle
They forget that a person does not
change his creations just because he
is successful
They forget that this is one of the
things for which every artist strives

Why can't these same people
share your happiness as
they shared your struggle?

Why do I write?
I write because
I see something
or touch something
or smell something
or feel something
that I can not understand
until I try to describe it
in written
words.

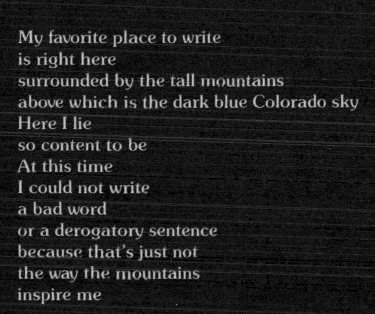

My favorite place to write
is right here
surrounded by the tall mountains
above which is the dark blue Colorado sky
Here I lie
so content to be
At this time
I could not write
a bad word
or a derogatory sentence
because that's just not
the way the mountains
inspire me

I honestly believe that if
everyone only had the chance to
lie here quietly
admiring the scenery
there would be no more
destruction
because this kind of
peace envelops
our entire being
If only everyone had
this chance

Music touches feelings
that words can not.
It is the melody
of the heart,
the voice
of the Spirit.
It inspires some
to think of the past,
some to create
and some to cry.

Music makes me
love.

Children
of nature

Come into the mountains, dear friend
Leave society and take no one with you
but your true self
Get close to nature
Your everyday games will be insignificant
Notice the clouds
spontaneously forming patterns
and try to do that with your life

Peace flows
from the sky
through the air
to me.

The fluffy pearl clouds
move from one pine tree
to another
high above the rocky mountains.

The birds' singing
brings me out of my trance
to remind me of life
and who I am.

I am a
very tiny
tiny
part of the world.
A part that
is lucky enough
to be able to
touch the beauty
of nature.

Colorado
where the mountains reign
and the dry clear air
makes one always want to
be outside

Colorado
a place to be whoever you want
there is no style to follow
no symbols needed to prove yourself

Colorado
land of horses
and cows
and people
just happy to be alive

Colorado
land of the sun
mountain of peace

I left the mountains
for a trip to the city
Oh — the lights
the restaurants
the theaters
the people
the action

It was fun
but not nearly as much
as coming home
to the mountains

Beautiful green and yellow weed,
they say to cut you down quickly
before you spread throughout the neighborhood.

You look just like a flower to me,
only a little stronger.
Don't feel bad because they call you
a health hazard.
Feel sad that they are so prejudiced.
You know they are like that with people, too.

I will never cut you down.
I want a garden of weeds.
Please spread your seedlings densely,
and thank you for making the ground enchanted.

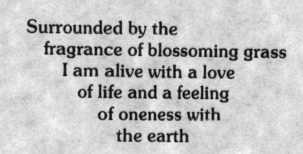

Surrounded by the
fragrance of blossoming grass
I am alive with a love
of life and a feeling
of oneness with
the earth

I stare at the sky
and wonder why
why have we made such a mess of things

How could we tear up the seas
use up all the trees
all in the name of progress

I close my eyes
my love and I
with dreams of flowers and trees
admiring the leaves
nature is beautiful
love is ecstatic

Now is the time to
enjoy these things

The ocean brought me peace
the wind gave me energy
the sun warmed my spirit
the flowers showed me life
but you made me feel
                    love

It is so nice being with you
Somehow the grass feels softer
and the birds seem to sing just for us

The world is warmer
when one has someone to hide with

Our special spot
where the clear sky forms a roof
over the greens and browns
nature's unplanned blending

The peaceful singing of the birds
makes us forget the world outside
and I only want to live in this environment
with our love as pure and beautiful
as nature surrounding us

The crickets
sing
and the ants
dance.
The marmots
sing
and the rocks
dance.
The birds
sing
and the leaves
dance.

And I sit
in the grass
so lucky
to hear this
magnificent
symphony.

The sand looks out on the rippling water
The sky has cast an omnipotent dimness
Each wave crashes against the shore
washing the shells to mingle with the pebbles

We are so tiny
Staring at the ocean
I wonder what other than
nature is significant

Let us dance in the sun
wearing wild flowers in our hair
And let us huddle together
as darkness takes over

We are at home amidst the
                birds and the trees
        for we are
        children of nature

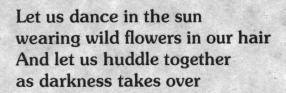

I'm not
that kind
of girl

THE NEW WOMAN

The new woman arises
full of confidence
she speaks eloquently
and thinks independently

Full of strength
she organizes efficiently
and directs proudly

She is the new woman
capable of changing
the course
of society

Don't ever say wife to me
it's too cold
if someone asks who I am
tell them I am the one you love
if they quiver, "Are you married?"
then say that we are sharing our lives together.

"Can you type?"

"No!"

"Can you file?"

"No!"

"Can you take shorthand?"

"No!"

"How about simple bookkeeping?"

"No!"

"What on earth can you do?"

"Everything you can!"

When I become a young mother,
will my life be centered in the kitchen?
Will I listen to the day's activities of my family
and have nothing to say about mine?
Will I dream about a career I could have had?
Will I lose my creativity
and become bored with life?
When I become a young mother,
why can't I live the life I did before?

DO IT NOW SISTER

After my babies grow up, I'm going to
grow my hair long again
and buy new clothes for myself.
I'm going to go to Europe
and meet all kinds of people.
I'm going to go back to school
and finish my degree.
I'm going to start my career in
social work.
I used to want all these things
before I had my babies.
After my children grow up,
I'll become a person again.

I don't want to be a Secretary
I should be a President

I don't want to be a Bookkeeper
I should be the Accountant

I don't want to be a Gal Friday
I should be the General Manager

I don't want to be a Saleswoman
I should be the Marketing Manager

I don't want to be a Switchboard Operator
I should be the Communications Coordinator

Instead of being an Assembly Checker
I ought to be the Quality Control Technician

Instead of being an Alteration Lady
I ought to be a Tailor

Instead of being a Midwife
I ought to be an Obstetrician

Instead of being a Cook
I ought to be a Chef

I don't want to be a Secretary
I should be a President

I want to laugh
I want to cry

I am aggressive
I am shy

I feel strong
I feel weak

I feel confident
I feel meek

I look pretty
I look bad

I feel happy
I feel sad

I am love
I am hate

I act crazy
I act straight

I feel soft
I feel tough

I feel sexy
I feel rough

Many emotions amidst each day
together with reason are what guide my way

What kind of person am I?
Am I good?
Am I kind?
Am I honest?
Am I loving?
Do I have talents?
Am I smart?
You should judge me on
these things;
but, that I am a woman
tells you nothing.

How could you have the
nerve to say
"No woman of mine will have a career"
Do you realize what you are saying
You are saying that you are superior
You can have a career
but your woman must sit quietly at home
You are saying that you can be around people
but your woman must speak only to children
You are saying that you can be stimulated by events
but your woman must be stimulated from washing
        the floor
You are saying that if
your woman has a career
you would no longer be the total center
of everything your woman does
You are saying that your woman
must deteriorate
(you know that is what will happen if
you don't let her use her mind)
You are saying
that your woman must have no goals of her own
that your woman must have no ideas of her own
that your woman must have no life of her own

You are a murderer

THANKS, MOM

Since I had a mother
whose many interests
kept her excited and occupied

Since I had a mother
who interacted with so many people
that she had a real feeling for the world

Since I had a mother
who always was strong
through any period of suffering

Since I had a mother
who was a complete person
I always had a model
to look up to
and that made it easier
for me to develop into
an independent woman

What is it
in a woman
that causes her
to be so full of life
ideas and excitement
when young
but right after marriage
to lose all interests
and all capabilities
outside of
keeping house and
seeing that her
husband is fit

Is it the fault
of the husbands
whose careers and
egos must be nurtured
to the point where the
woman has
no energy left for
herself

Or is it the fault
of society
which trains the woman
that the most important
thing she can do
is to get a successful man
and that the woman
needn't develop
her own mind and
activities once this
goal is reached

Or is it the fault
of the woman
who sees
the world outside
and what it has
done to her father
and her husband
and she takes
the easy way out
by not joining the world

Though each woman
has a different
reason for her decay
we all need to
overcome the reason and
overcome the cause and
immediately seek
an interesting
life of our own

Well dear mate
Why are you so late
Whom did you talk to
What did you do
Were you alone
So many hours away from me
I'm lonely, can't you see

Please dear beau
Let me know
With whom did you speak
With whom did you meet
With whom did you dine
What papers did you sign
So many hours away from me
I'm lonely, can't you see

AN EDUCATION?

"What do you want to be when you grow up?"
the teacher asked her pupils.
"A fireman," Nelson answered.
"A policeman," yelled Robert.
"A nurse," said Myra.
"A baseball player," shouted Michael.
"A mother," answered Sonia.
"An airplane pilot," whispered Baby girl.

Everyone in the class laughed at Baby girl.
"Did you ever see a girl pilot?" yelled Bob.
"Well it is possible. All I have to do is
learn to fly real well," defended Baby girl.
"Girls aren't supposed to fly airplanes. Only
boys are pilots; right, teacher?" asked Mike.
"Well boys and girls, I must admit that I
have never seen a woman airplane pilot. Didn't
you once say that you wanted to be a teacher,
Baby girl?" asked the teacher.
"No, I always wanted to be a pilot,"
claimed Baby girl.
"See Baby girl," the teacher sermonized,
"most girls work only a few years after they
are done with school. Then they get married
and spend all their time raising a family."
"Yeah, girls are too stupid to be airplane
pilots," shouted Nelson.
"Well how come I get all A's, and you get
all C's?" asked Baby girl proudly.

BABY GIRL GETS IT FROM ALL ENDS

Baby girl is born!
Pink pajamas,
Pink booties,
and a pink bonnet
to make her look like
a sweet little princess.

Baby girl's fifth birthday,
and lots of dolls,
and doll clothes,
and little furniture
for Baby girl's doll house.
"Of course she likes these toys,
and besides, it's good training for
later in life."

Baby girl's knees keep getting bruised
and she asks to be allowed to wear
slacks to school.
Mother says, "Of course not.
No other girl does, and if
you'd stop being a tomboy, you wouldn't
keep falling. It almost serves you right."
"What is a tomboy?" Baby girl asks her mother.
"It's a girl who likes boys' games rather than girls' games,"
answers Mother.
"What's a boy's game?" Baby girl queries.
"Climbing trees, football, you know, anything wild."
"I want to play exciting games like the boys do,"
Baby girl yells.
"They wouldn't even let you play because you're much
weaker than they are," assured mother.
"No I'm not. Today I beat up Michael, and he's the
strongest boy in the class!" said Baby girl proudly.

Those in love
must remain complete people
first unto themselves
and then to each other

Today I woke up
feeling strange
but special.
For the first time
in my life
I thought about the fact that I
could produce a baby.
Out of me
from he
a little baby.
Unbelievable.

Sure all my friends
have had babies
but I never thought of myself
as a man's wife
or a child's mother.
I am just me, leading
my own life
and in love with he.

But today, I pictured
a little baby building sand castles
and it belonged to us.

I am a
city woman,
aggressive and independent.
I wear the latest fashions
to my Broadway office.
I romance with
actors, lawyers and executives;
I've been with many men.
I see my psychoanalyst once a week;
and if I have spare time,
I go to art museums and read the New York Times.
I eat out
and sleep five hours a night.
I move very fast
and every minute of my day and night is occupied.
I am a
city woman
who dreams a lot
about the country.

We are women-people
free to do what we want
live the way we choose
look the way we like
say the way we feel

You must all accept this

You want the kind of girl who
fixes your clothes
cooks your food
and cleans your house
while waiting for you to
come home from work

You want the kind of girl
whom your friends will call fun
and your boss will call pretty
and whom you may call your very own

You want the kind of girl
who looks and feels perfect
who admires you
and who listens to you in awe

You want the kind of girl
who gives up her career
to help you succeed in yours
and who gives up her whole being
to make you a superman

Well honey
I'm proud to say that
I'm not that kind of girl

**Susan and Stephen
July, 1976**

Susan Polis Schutz

Stephen Schutz

Susan began writing at age seven
when she put together a handwritten
newspaper in Peekskill, N.Y., and
to the delight of millions of readers,
she's been writing ever since. In a
simple but poignant style, Susan
writes without rhyme — but with all the
reason in the world. Writing about
her feelings on her natural surround-
ings, people, love and social change,
Susan is endowed with a love of nature
and life that she has shared with
countless others.

After growing up in Peekskill, Susan
went to Rider College in New Jersey
where she earned degrees in
English and biology. Although she
taught school in Harlem for several

years while attending graduate school, she continued to write, free-lancing for newspapers and magazines. During this time, she met and later married Stephen Schutz.

Stephen, raised in the Bronx, attended New York's High School of Music and Art, a specialized school where he learned the basics of drawing, photography and calligraphy. His study of art became over-shadowed by physics books and lab tables at M.I.T. and Princeton (where he earned a Ph.D. in theoretical physics in 1970), but it surfaced again after moving to Colorado for post-doctoral work. Because of a phenomenal demand for Susan's poetry and Stephen's illustrations, he gave up his career in physics and went back to the drawing board — literally.

Interwoven with Stephen's line drawings and airbrush blends, Susan's poetry creates a music all its own. The harmony of their love, sensitivity and universal appeal emanating from their mountain home is heard in all directions of the globe. The Schutzes are recognized as the best-selling poet-artist team in the English-speaking countries of the world.

As John Alexander of the *Saturday Evening Post* remarks, Susan and Stephen are ". . . friends you want to know and to speak with more."